Skiing Fitness

Max Rieder/Martin Fiala

Skiing Fitness

Conditioning Training for Ski Sports

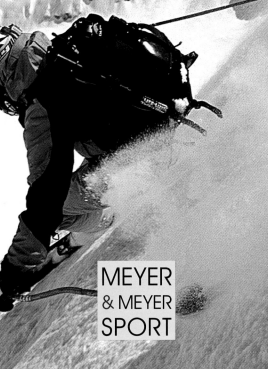

MEYER
& MEYER
SPORT

British Library Cataloguing in Publication Data
A catalogue record for this book is available from the British Library

Skiing Fitness
Condition Training for Ski Sports / Max Rieder; Martin Fiala.
– Oxford : Meyer und Meyer, 2006
ISBN 10: 1-84126-173-4
ISBN 13: 978-1-84126-173-7

© 2006 by Meyer & Meyer Sport (UK) Ltd.
Aachen, Adelaide, Auckland, Budapest, Graz, Johannesburg,
New York, Olten (CH), Oxford, Singapore, Toronto
Member of the World
Sports Publishers' Association (WSPA)
www.w-s-p-a.org
Printed and bound by: TZ Verlag, Germany
ISBN 10: 1-84126-173-4
ISBN 13: 978-1-84126-173-7
E-Mail: verlag@m-m-sports.com
www.m-m-sports.com

CONTENTS

I FOREWORDS

Martina Ertl – World Champion

"To enter the winter season in good shape is an important foundation for an enjoyable and successful ski season. I, too, have to do my preparation, mainly in summer and autumn, so that I am able to smile when I cross the finish line in winter. As I like to smile, I always take care with my preparation."

Hilda Gerg – Olympic Champion

"Conditioning training has become more and more important in the last few years. It is no longer sufficient to do a little "recreational sport" during the summer; one must be specifically prepared for the demands of the winter ski season. Conditioning training forms a large part of these preparations. It is also important to carry out a well-coordinated conditioning program between competitions in the winter.

My main focus in the winter is on recovery sessions, so that I am well rested for training, and especially for competitions. For me, recovery is not just "lazing around" in the sauna or going for walks. The recovery sessions, whether for strength training, speed or endurance, are all very light. This enables me to maintain the performance level that I worked hard to reach in the summer, but doesn't leave me too tired to ski well.

In addition, a relaxed jog in the forest is also a great opportunity to unwind mentally, and to get myself ready for the next day.

For me, conditioning training in the winter is a nice change, albeit a necessary one, so that I can always start races in good shape and avoid injuries or falls."

Regina Häusl – Downhill-Combined Cup Champion

"For me, physical fitness is the most important thing in skiing. In order to get through the ski season without getting injured, it is vital to start in the autumn to lay the necessary foundations for the winter months. To wait to start conditioning on the slopes is very dangerous. Skiing is only really fun if you still have breath to yodel even during your last runs!"

Christian Neureuther – Ex-Slalom Star

"Of course, all skiers are fit, but the fittest always win! Ski sports offer unbelievable dimensions for everyone, but they are only attainable with physical and mental fitness. That is why it is so important to read this book."

II   INTRODUCTION

Whether you are old, young, a good or bad skier, a free skier, telemarker or racer, and trying to identify the reason why skiing is so attractive, it will be hard to figure out exactly why. For some, it is the speed, for others just to be out there in nature; some are excited by the mental or physical challenge, the group dynamic, and others again for the ego trip, the risk, the perfection, the success, the fun...

All these answers seem very different at first, maybe even a little crazy! But if you look and listen more closely, you often notice a happy satisfied mood in those interviewed. They gesticulate wildly; their eyes shine; the palms of their hands get damp, and their thighs get warm.

This book is not intended to find out WHY skiing is so fascinating, for we do not want to and cannot reduce this unique winter pleasure to that level. Instead, we want to provide a fitness and training guide to enable you to experience both the fascination of skiing in winter more safely, faster and more intensively, and to enjoy the way the conditioning process enriches your daily life.

The top skiers know only too well that they must be exceptionally physically fit to be able to produce the correct technique in extreme situations, to get from A to B as fast as possible. They also know that being in tip-top physical shape is the best life insurance policy.

It doesn't matter whether your goal is to win a classic downhill race, to ski down from the crag that has been too high for you up until now, to do your first 720 Misty Flip, to leave behind the most beautiful trail in the virgin snowy slope, or just to get through a skiing vacation without aching muscles or injuries, being fitter makes it easier to achieve. We bet you that you will notice a few other pleasant side effects, too!

III THE HOLISTIC PHILOSOPHY OF FITNESS AND TRAINING IN SKI SPORTS

The various forms of ski sports have grown more and more diverse in the past few years. The boundaries between the different disciplines are blurred as many skiers often practice several types of skiing.

But what has the refining of different ways of getting down "to the valley" really changed? We believe that the diversification has provided many new opportunities to practice ski sports in a more individual way. We believe that nearly everyone can find a very personal reason for the fascination they feel outside on the slopes.

"Rebirth" of Telemarking

Recently, the motto "free your heel and your mind will follow" has come to express a newly discovered passion for Telemarking. In the early 1990s, Telemarkers were still regarded as a little eccentric; these days, Telemarkers can be found in abundance in almost every ski resort, indulging their love of the earliest form of skiing. Many take themselves out to backcountry skiing on the pristine slopes; others go wild in the halfpipe, or the funpark, or go carving on prepared tracks.

Free Skiing

Free skiing used to be practiced only by backcountry skiers. However, more and more often, the way from the peak is not just the way to the valley, but a test of what is possible, an expression of personality, a thrill, and a sporting challenge. Whether you go to the top by lift, heli, or on foot, the line, jumps, style, as well as a mixture of risk, enjoyment and self-discovery characterize the descent.

Carving

The discussion as to whether carving was originally a form of skiing, and was then refined by snowboarders, or whether it was actually invented by snowboarders, can go on for hours! It is certainly true that carving, and the shaped parabolic skis used for it are in any case a real improvement, not just for the industry, but for all skiers, and every single ski discipline is now unthinkable without them. Radical and tight curves, being able to perform tight radii without side-slipping, extreme banking and high centrifugal force, with or without ski poles,... these areaddictive movements!

Are carving skis really so dangerous? Do the rounded, shortened parabolic skis really mean that the skier is more quickly exposed to extreme G-forces, and therefore loses control of the skis more quickly? Empirical evidence shows that the use of the new skis is not linked to a higher risk of accidents – at least not at the recreational level.

At the elite level, it is a different story. The discussion about the safety of carving skis is mainly fueled by the frequent and spectacular falls by racing skiers. Actually, the new skis have brought top skiers even closer to their limits. A quite different technique, similar to that for the giant slalom, makes it possible to take a much more direct line, and yet to ski completely without side-slipping and therefore without losing speed.

Are these risks transferable to grass roots skiing? We don't think so. Their shortness makes carving skis easier to turn for inexperienced skiers, and therefore also safer. In addition, it is quite obvious that many skiers own the new skis, but have not mastered the skill of skiing on the edge, as it is actually quicker but cannot be learned overnight. It is precisely the diversity of the demands which make the sport so fascinating, and yet so challenging.

Before we deal with the subject of this book, fitness training, in depth, we would really like to present all the parameters that affect the sport of skiing.

Equipment

Equipment has evolved rapidly in recent years. The advantages of the new ski model make it easier for most skiers to have fun. It's not just skis that have changed though: bindings, ski shoes, sunglasses and clothing have also improved greatly.

Safety bindings, more stable ski shoes, lighter ski poles, defogging sunglasses and warm, waterproof and breathable clothing material make for safer and easier enjoyment of nature. However, make sure you choose the correct equipment.

Weather

Skiing is mainly practiced outdoors (recently also in indoor skiing centers). We cannot manipulate the weather yet, thank goodness! We do have to learn to weigh it subjectively as good as possible, though. The behavior and properties of the snow, temperatures, air and snow humidity, visibility and wind direction are individual parameters that have an influence on each other and inevitably affect our skiing experience.

People

Last of all, we are adventurers who want to enjoy skiing. All our abilities affect how well we ski, and in turn, our performance affects our abilities.

 ### Mental State
A combination of mental abilities that include fear, courage, risk, confidence and self-awareness, and therefore success and failure, fun and torture.

 ### The Cognitive Abilities
The ability to filter an abundance of information, and to modify behavior according to perceptions.

Technical Abilities
The visible ability to use the correct skiing technique for each different situation that comes up on the slopes.

Tactical Abilities

These abilities include conscious decisions concerning the choice of line, of risk, the selection of equipment...

 ## Physical Abilities

These components include strength, speed, endurance, coordination, flexibility and conditioning.

This is all complicated by the fact that nearly all these factors are interdependent, and influence each other either directly or indirectly. If you realize this, it becomes clear that physical performance or enjoyment can only be as great as the weakest link in this structure. It means that, ideally, all factors should be covered according to each person's goals.

Which abilities are the most important though? There is no single answer to this question as it can vary according to each person's existing state of fitness and their goals. However, physical fitness would seem to us to be the most universal both in terms of its influence on other abilities, and in terms of its usefulness in everyday life.

The reduction of fitness to the function of a multi-purpose vehicle does not seem to us to be sufficient though to maintain motivational levels for regular, long-term training. We prefer to think that getting fit and keeping fit is a way of life, like skiing itself. A path towards a goal, with many enjoyable experiences and surprises along the way, that is definitely worth taking.

IV CONDITIONING PREPARATION FOR SKI SPORTS

Profile of Conditioning Demands and Performance Indicators in Ski Sports

The diversity of the range of recreational winter sports mentioned above means that the preparation requirements are also very different for each sport. Unlike other popular sports, skiing makes demands in nearly all aspects of fitness.

⇨ Endurance
It should be kept in mind that loading is not limited just to the duration of the runs. The time spent in the cold winter environment, and the usually unfamiliar altitude use up a great deal of energy, and thereby increase the total load on the body. Good endurance also helps the body tackle the last runs, and to face the next day refreshed and ready to go.

⇨ Strength
In elite sports, short-term loads of up to 800kg have been measured during turn movements. These forces act on the whole body, not just on the legs. Good core stability is just as important as having powerful thighs.

⇨ Speed
Good basic speed enables you to control your skis in all situations. The correct technique is also required, of course, but you can always react more safely and quickly if you have the necessary basic speed to enable movements to be performed rapidly and correctly.

⇨ Flexibility

As in nearly all sports, flexibility increases the range of movement and makes more movements possible. Good flexibility also protects against injury.

⇨ Coordination

Skiing involves complex movement sequences at all levels and speeds, included in a variable downward motion with diverse conditions, over varying terrain, interacting with physical, mental, cognitive and technical variables. In short, skiing is hard work, but fascinating!

The conditioning and coordination demands alone vary enormously in the different events in the Alpine World Cup. For example, the time requirement (up to 2.5 minutes) means that a downhill skier has to have completely different endurance and strength requirements as opposed to a slalom skier, who "only" has to prepare for a load lasting about 50 seconds. However, these special demands are increased if one wants to be the best. The coordination demands are also very complex and diverse. Proof of this is the smaller and smaller number of skiers who are capable of competing successfully in all skiing disciplines.

Appropriate training for skiing is very varied and develops a very versatile, and functionally-trained athlete with none of the great weaknesses that can be seen in other sports.

It is not for nothing that skiing stars come off best in discipline comparisons. For example, Kjetill-Andre Aamodt can easily do the splits, and just as easily do a forward flip from a standing position. All good skiers are capable of tightrope walking or riding a monocycle, and it is not uncommon for them to be outdone only by bobsledders or weightlifters in the strength department.

These performance indicators are based on different personal goals and different personal preconditions; they always require individual requirement profiles.

It is not our intention in this book to take you to your physical limits. We also doubt whether a general guide like this one is really useful in terms of peak performance for everyone, as in the process of becoming the best, each person's situation is so different. We would prefer to give you a few basic tips and ideas to get ready for the winter. Hopefully, you will find new exercises and approaches to training, which will motivate you to start the coming winter in better shape. If this book manages to prepare you better for the winter, we will have achieved our goal!

Practical Training Implications

As you can see from the requirement profile, and the many different types of ski sports available today, the implications for practical training are very complex. Because this book is very practically oriented, we focus on the practical training implications for every coach and athlete, and not the theoretical background. So, the contents and training programs for elite level sports are adapted for large target groups to provide good quality training for as many skiers as possible.

Fig. 1 : Control Loop for Periodization

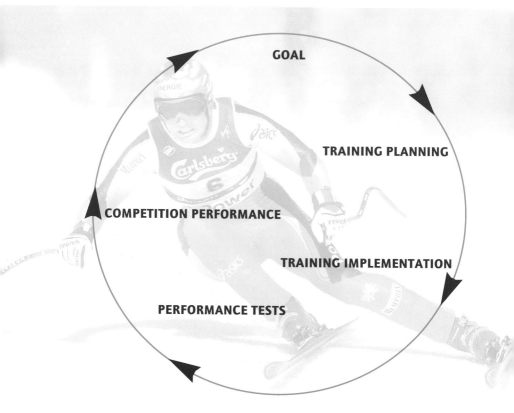

GOAL

TRAINING PLANNING

COMPETITION PERFORMANCE

TRAINING IMPLEMENTATION

PERFORMANCE TESTS

Periodization

Periodization is a vital part of modern training. It is the way to be in top shape for the most important competition at the elite level.

Training is divided into phases, and each phase has a goal. The aim is to incorporate the planned training content, exercises and methods, into the different training blocks in the best way possible. Performance tests and almost daily performance analysis enable training to be adapted as well as possible to the current state of fitness of the athlete. There are recovery sessions, and load and recovery rhythms must be respected, so that individual performance may be improved more and more, and the desired competition performances may be achieved.

These principles are very important for successful conditioning for keeping fit in general, as well as for skiing in particular. They are the basic training principles for every athlete.

Training Goals

At the advanced level, goals set are often deciding factors; they also hold for every training athlete, too, though. There are many possible goals in skiing:

General Goals can include:
- Finishing a day's skiing without feeling too tired.
- Taking a very difficult descent in one's stride.
- Doing fun carving curves without losing power.

Specific Goals can include:
- Achieving age-appropriate conditioning parameters (strength, speed, endurance).
- Learning specific coordination exercises, such as gymnastic exercises or balancing exercises.

It is important in both cases that training plans and programs are adapted to reflect these goals. At the advanced and elite level, it is absolutely essential to make training goals correspond to individual circumstances and current performance level. You should analyze your own strengths and weaknesses, and see goals as the way to reach higher and higher standards, even the very top. The principle that the skier should have no weaknesses in any of the many requirements should be the foundation for the skier's conditioning training goals. An athlete who has excellent endurance ability, but little ability to transfer motor strength, or poor movement technique cannot be considered to have the ideal conditioning level for a skier. A skier should possess balanced, all-around abilities in every area of performance. So, when setting goals, weaknesses should be strengthened and strengths consolidated, and this requires systematic and honest evaluation.

The training plan is based on the training goals. For successful conditioning training, here are a few final practical tips relating to the setting of training goals:

⇨   Set realistic, achievable goals. It is very important to take into account the time available for training.

⇨   Goals must firstly be geared to the improvement of performance; other secondary goals can be:

   ❑   I will enjoy training more.

   ❑   I would like to find the right balance for work, ski sports and family.

   ❑   I would like to do something to improve my body and personal well-being every day, even if just for a few minutes.

   ❑   I will always be looking out for new exercises and new training runs, etc.

The goal is an end in itself, but the road to the goal can also be a goal in itself. Motivation is what enables us to reach our goals.

Training Planning

For the active skier, any kind of training plan is both the tool that enables them to achieve their training goals, and also their training manual.

There is a difference between long-term training plans, like the overall training plans for elite level squads, annual training plans, training phases or periodic plans, and macrocycles that usually last from several weeks to a maximum of three months. The smallest sub-division in a training plan is called a training session.

The longer the plan lasts, the more abstract and general the contents are. The shorter the plan, the more precise and exact the contents should be. The most important planning period for the target group of this book is the weekly plan, or the training session with corresponding training programs. Several examples of weekly training plans for different groups are listed in Chapter 5. In practical training terms, it is as vital for advanced athletes as it is for recreational skiers and young beginners that plans are corrected and adapted on an ongoing basis to the athlete's current circumstances, such as physical and mental state, and work or study commitments.

The best training plan in the world is useless if it is too hard to stick to. A cornerstone for enjoyable and successful performance improvement is developing a "feeling for training" (feeling for demands, for pace and physical awareness...) especially for athletes who would like to improve their fitness for ski sports without really aspiring to perform at a high level.

The training session can vary from between 30 minutes for relaxation or flexibility and several hours for long basic endurance sessions. The all-around demands of ski sports mean that a coordination warm-up and cool-down are very important. At the advanced level, do a few coordination exercises (fartlek running, different kinds of jumps, exercises to improve balance, stride rate drills like tapping or skipping, etc...) after endurance or strength sessions to develop both the motor skills and the musculature, which over the long term will contribute towards a very high movement level.

Conditioning Preparation

The usual warm-up activities such as jogging, running, coordination exercises, stretching and flexibility, and general strengthening exercises should become automatic, and must be included in every training session.

Activities like loose jogging and running, stretching and flexibility exercises, yoga-type exercises, and body relaxation exercises are good for cooling down. The recreational athlete should always bear in mind that the warm up should activate the mind and motivation, as well as the body. If possible, the two hemispheres of the brain should work together in every training session, so that you feel good about the training and your body.

An example for a weekly plan in June/July/August is set out below:

Target Group: About four training sessions per week to get fit for the winter, with no pretensions to high level competition.

EXAMPLE OF A WEEKLY PLAN

Day/Date	Type of trainings (Place)	Training content (exercises – load)	Notes/Observations
Mon.	Basic Endurance – Mountain Bike circuits in the mountains.	Basic Endurance II – Development endurance zone with strength endurance, about 90 min. Pulse rate 145-175 bpm	Downhill, ensure good downhill technique. Have fun.
Tues.	Free or other sport		
Wed.	Strength – Basic weight training for several muscle groups combined with strengthening and balance	Exhaustion Principle: 12-15 reps. 4-6 sets, average speed, see basic program legs and upper body as circuit. Always include balancing exercises between the strength exercises. About 120-180 min.	Gymnastics and flexibility exercises as cool down, include trunk strengthening exercises in warm-up.
Thurs.	Free or speed coordination sport, e.g. tennis, ball game or inline skating etc.		
Fri.	Strength – speed strength with coordination and speed exercises	2-3 exercises for the legs speed strength training about 40-60% load, fast and reactive, about 8-10 reps. or about 20 seconds, with jump sequence, imitation exercises	Warm up well and ensure best technique and fast movement speed.
Sat.	Basic Endurance on bike or running or hiking, possibly include intervals	Basic Endurance I-II, possibly with 3-5 extensive intervals (e.g. 5 x 1 min.). Session lasts several hours. Pulse rate up to 160 (180 during intervals)	
Sun.	Free or alternative sport or power yoga, stretching and strengthening exercises for core stability, recovery run	About 60 min.	Holistic approach to life. Set goals for following week.

Training Implementation and Organization

Ski sports are some of the most complex sports around. Conditioning and fitness training lay the foundations both for fast times, and better results, and for safer skiing, and more enjoyment during the winter.

Ski sports training is organized, so that it is always possible to throw in a short training session for core stability or coordination exercises for balance, or to improve general and specific movement skills.

Ski sports are certainly some of the most spectacular and dynamic sports. The training and the training ideas should be carried out in the same euphoric and dynamic spirit.

Here are some tips for effective conditioning and fitness training for ski sports:

⇨ Focus on all-around training and varied content.

⇨ Systematically combine general training (basic endurance, muscle building, stability training,...) with specific training (special coordination exercises, speed strength, and strength endurance training).

⇨ For focused high level training, you need to train certain content, like strength ability and endurance ability in intensive blocks to significantly improve performance.

⇨ In training sessions containing different elements, speed or motor skill elements should be carried out at the beginning of the training session.

⇨ All-around training also involves complex load and adaptation mechanisms, i.e. recovery times must be determined by holistic well-being (physical sensations, motivational state, etc.) not just the purely physical.

⇨ The emphasis should be on having fun.

Training Content, Methods and Exercises

The general training theory, and the findings of modern sports science, together with the findings from competitive sports, show us almost daily how training can be made more effective by incorporating such and such an exercise, or by following such and such a method. There are plenty of publications that give information about newer and more effective ways to train. Every type of conditioning has its own methods, e.g. endurance or interval methods for endurance, muscle building, maximal strength, muscle performance, or strength endurance methods in the strength area, repetition methods or series interval methods in coordination or speed training. As this book focuses on the practical side of training, and on making it enjoyable, these theories are deliberately avoided in this chapter, and described instead in Chapter 5 in the training programs for each type of conditioning. We would now like to present clear descriptions of the contents of each one with the corresponding methods and exercises. The following points are summarized below as training tips:

⇨   The combination of training volume, training intensity and the recovery structure make up the training method. The greater the training volume, the more basic it is (basic endurance, basic strength). The more intensive the training, the more specific the training effects (specific anaerobic endurance, maximal strength).

⇨   Training volume and intensity compensate each other mutually, i.e. the more intensive the training, the lower the training volume, and the greater the training volume, the lower the load. High volume and high intensity training is reserved for top athletes only.

⇨   Training volumes and intensities are products of the duration of a training session, of stats, e.g. speed or pulse rate, of the additional load with the corresponding movement speed, of the distance or load times completed, the repetitions and sets, the length and structure of recovery breaks.

⇨   Training methods are mostly equally valid, but not every training method is effective for optimal individual training. Individual training experiences can often be more effective than pre-determined standards.

Training and Performance Testing

Modern training means testing. In pure endurance sports (running, mountain biking, cycling, cross-country skiing...) or pure strength sports, the analysis of performance data is absolutely vital, and is very often communicated to the athlete during training.

In ski sports, where a great variety of conditioning factors can contribute to a skier's performance, not all performance data are immediately available. However, looking at the world's top skiers, we can see that their strength endurance, complex coordination, and maximal strength were or are well above average.

Performance tests in competitive sports are biomechanical or sports medicine procedures that are used to measure strength, speed, flexibility and endurance. In terms of training for fitness and for up and coming skiers, sport-motor tests are often sufficient to establish performance levels in the various abilities.

The feeling for the body and performance mentioned above are a good way to evaluate training and performance, too, for you should only test your performance if you are really focused and motivated.

The table on the following page shows a small selection of possible sport-motor tests for general fitness.

OVERVIEW OF SIMPLE TEST

Test	Test Description
Lateral Balancing Test	On a taut tightrope about 5m long or on a balance pole, walk forward and backward (1 minute) or set paths, e.g. 4 paths (2 attempts).
Balance test forward/backward	On a taut tightrope about 5m long or a balance pole, stand sideways in the ski position for 30 seconds to 2 minutes according to performance level (2 attempts).
Strength test - Leg Extensor Musculature	In the leg press or e.g. also with medium 90° squats, with an average load of about 50-60% of maximal load, do as many reps. as possible.
Strength test – Front and rear Upper Body	Bench press or bench pulls with average load 50-60% of maximal load, do as many reps. as possible.
Leg specific strength endurance	Maintain ski position (about 90° knee angle) on a balance board for as long as possible.
Speed strength or speed strength endurance	Complete a series of two-footed jumps over about 20 cm high hurdles for 20 seconds, possibly 40 seconds (Speed strength endurance) as fast as possible.
Complex core muscles	Complete a core stability circuit of 4-6 exercises for abs, oblique abs, back, side, bottom, whole body tension with 30-50 reps.., or for 1 min. for static exercises.
General endurance test: cycling, mountain biking or running	Several variations: Run 3000m on the track, trail or mountain over a set distance, mountain bike or bike mountain time trial or set distance. Conduct a load increase test with a bike ergometer (e.g. increase from 50 Watts in 25 or 50 Watt increments) or treadmill (e.g. from 8 km/h in 2 km/h increments). Each step lasts 3 min.

SELECTED CONDITIONING ABILITIES IN SKI SPORTS

Abilities	Values, Performance, Notes
Keeping balance, mainly lateral	+ / 0 / - Scale: + = accomplished, high level 0 = partly accomplished, average level - = not accomplished, low level, time stopped or distance measured
Keeping balance, mainly forward/backward	+ / 0 / - Scale: + = accomplished, high level 0 = partly accomplished - = not accomplished, low level, time stopped
Strength-endurance muscle performance of the leg extension musculature, also involves the trunk musculature, e.g. in the case of weaknesses in the trunk area.	Number of valid reps.. in a series without stopping between individual reps..
Strength endurance muscle performance of the upper body musculature e.g. chest, lats and arms, plus trunk musculature	Number of valid reps. in a series without stopping between individual reps.
Specific strength endurance abilities of the leg musculature at a typical working angle	Time of correct execution of the test in minutes and seconds
Reactive speed strength abilities of the legs with relatively high coordination precision demands	Number of valid reps. in the set time
Whole trunk musculature	+ / 0 / - Scale + = accomplished, high level 0 = partly accomplished, average level - = not accomplished, low level
Basic aerobic endurance with specific anaerobic endurance abilities	Completed time with pulse rate check, in the load increase test completed time with pulse rate check

Training Documentation

The last part of this chapter deals with the documentation of training, which is interesting for the amateur and competitive skier and essential for top athletes. This is the only way to see whether the planned training has actually been done, or the current circumstances have been adapted to. At the end of the day it is not the planned training, but the accomplished training that matters.

For ski sports, training documentation is necessary to give an overall picture due to the varied nature of the training content. A typical training diary can be found in a software form, e.g. from POLAR, or in a home-made form, which is often more practical.

The table on the following page shows a blank template from a weekly training diary for the junior competitive level.

WEEKLY TRAINING DAY

Day/ Date	Training Content	Exercise – Load Time – Intensity – Amount	Comments
Mon.			
Tues.			
Wed.			
Thurs.			
Fri.			
Sat.			
Sun.			

Summary (Hours and minutes):

Basic strength Legs:...... Basic Strength Upper body ...... General Strength ....

Special speed strength/maximal strength .... Strength endurance..............

General speed/coordination ....Special speed strength/Coordination ....

Basic endurance ....Special endurance..............Recovery ....

Flexibility ....Games/sports ....Other ....

TOTAL:...........................

V TRAINING PRACTICE
- PROGRAM

This chapter deals with the practical side of training. We have tried to combine our years of experience as athletes and coaches with current ski sports trends. The main target groups of this book are children, schoolchildren and young people, but also ambitious skiers who want to improve. The exercises and programs are specifically selected for them. Alternative exercises, more advanced programs, detailed methods such as those used in daily training at the competitive level, are beyond the scope of this book. We have aimed for practicality and feasibility for a large number of people.

The ability to be trained is described at the start of every subchapter, along with descriptions of the most important methods, exercises and variations needed to carry out the training. Practical explanations are then given for selected training programs.

Strength Training

As you can see from the demand profile, ski sports are becoming more and more like athletic strength sports. It is impossible to use modern ski equipment correctly, and to master the modern ski technique without the appropriate specific strength. Upon analyzing a sample of World Cup skiers in the 2001/2002 season, the International Ski Federation (FIS) noted a 20% bodyweight increase compared with 12 years previously. This increase is mainly due to the increased strength arising from increased muscle mass.

Strength training in ski sports can be very varied by changing both the exercises and the methods. In any case, strength training should begin at the school age. You should start regular, light training of the large muscle groups before puberty when the most important basic strength exercises should also be learned.

As modern ski sports are whole body sports with greatly differing strength input, it is worth starting to look at strength training early on. In ski sports, the most important aspects of conditioning are strength training and special conditioning training. Competitive level athletes perform long strength training sessions, sometimes even twice a day.

Strength Training Methods

➡️ **Basic methods of increasing strength potential, building muscle and also improving muscle efficiency**

Repetitions/Time/Speed
❑   10 max. 20 reps. or about 30 seconds
❑   Average to quick movement speed
❑   Concentric and eccentric method
❑   Fluid reps, possibly also as increasing pyramid or increasing and decreasing with changing number of reps. and loads (pyramids with 15 – 10 – 8 – 10 – 15 reps.)

Intensity
❑   50 – 75% of maximal load

Sets/Rest/Training Structure
❑   4-6 sets with about 2-3 people
❑   active recovery (coordination exercises, shaking out...)

Main Muscle Groups
❑   All large muscle groups – the flexors and extensors of the legs, upper body and arms.

Implementation/Explanations
❑   The load/repetition ratio must be fully exploited for strength gain, i.e. if possible in every training set, the maximal number of reps. should be performed at each weight.
❑   The number of reps. should be adjusted to take into account loading increases between sets.
❑   Training can be carried out daily for alternating muscle groups.
❑   Try to do 2-3 training sessions per week to prepare for more intensive training
❑   12-14 year-olds should only do 1-2 sessions per week during preparation.

Supersets, without real rests, are a special variation for targeted muscle building. The rests are reduced to a minimum, and loads are usually reduced as well. Alternatively, reps. can be reduced; similar exercises for the same muscle groups are done one after the other. Forced reps. with the aid of a partner have their place in one phase of muscle building training. Such special methods do require greater strength training experience though.

⇨ **Strength training to improve special strength endurance in leg and trunk musculature**

Reps./Time/Speed
❑ About 30-50 reps. or about 30-90 seconds load

❑ Can extend to 3 minutes in special cases

❑ Static, quick and dynamic or also regulative and ski sport simulating movement sequences, according to the exercise.

Intensity
❑ About 25-45% of maximal load, according to the exercise, with just small additional loads or with bodyweight only

Sets/Rest/Training Structure
❑ 3-6 sets, in special cases up to 12 sets (e.g. in interval series)

❑ long rests 5-15 min.

❑ In the case of large additional loads, rest should be active, e.g. with light treadmill running

❑ Where additional loads are light, include some short rests, e.g. 30 second to 2 minutes

Main Muscle Groups
❑ Leg muscles, general strengthening for abs, back, trunk muscles or for all muscle groups.

Implementation/Explanations
- ❏ In competitive sports, this training method is usually used from the summer months to slowly get the body used to long and repeated loads.
- ❏ For junior and recreational athletes, it is a very effective method of preparing for the specific loads of winter sports.
- ❏ Motivation and strength of will are also developed.
- ❏ This training can also be carried out with very light loads in circuit training for large groups.
- ❏ The training can be performed 1-2 times per week.
- ❏ Sufficient recovery time should be planned to follow these training sessions.
- ❏ Excellent technique and movement should be focused on
- ❏ Be careful in the case of simultaneous highly intensive endurance loading or of inadequate basic endurance!

▷ **Speed strength and maximal strength methods to improve the specific speed strength and maximal strength of the leg musculature with strength, imitation and jumping exercises**

Reps./Time/Speed
- ❏ 5-8 reps. as fast as possible, loads last about 6 –15 seconds

Intensity
- ❏ For pronounced increase of maximal strength and intramuscular coordination with high loads (about 80-95% of maximal load)
- ❏ For a predominantly speed strength effect, about 3-50 % of maximal load
- ❏ No additional load in jumping and imitation exercises, but ensure maximal explosive movement

Sets/Rests/Structure
- ❏ About 5 sets, up to 8 sets in special cases
- ❏ Average to long rests, about 3-7 minutes
- ❏ Keep the speed-strength muscle feeling going during rests (isometric exercises, concentration)

Main Muscle Groups

❑　　This training is normally used in specific training for leg musculature in ski sports

Implementation/Explanations

❑　　In competitive sports, this is used in specific blocks 1-2 times per week, mainly in summer/autumn.

❑　　At recreational level, training is never performed with maximal load; speed strength training should be done with small loads and maximal movement speed.

❑　　Likewise for young people, where training without, loads but explosive movement is very important.

❑　　The training should be performed in a very well rested state, and you should aim for high muscle tension in the whole body, and for an absolutely correct technique.

Strength Training Exercises

Before we show you sample programs of training sessions, we would first of all like to give you a summary of the most important strength training exercises for ski sports. These include both general exercises that are also used for other sports, and ski specific exercises that are only used for ski sports.

A specific improvement in performance is only achievable by performing the so-called regulative strength exercises. These include popular exercises like squats, the ski position or lunges combined with regulative balancing exercises on balance devices, or "proprioception training equipment". This equipment can be balance boards, balance discs, pivot boards, soft rubber mats, Swiss ball or special balance equipment. These exercises are mainly used at competitive level, but are also suitable for use by recreational and junior athletes.

Exercises for all Leg Musculature

❏   High Squats, both legs
❏   Low Squats, both legs, with bar on chest or shoulders
❏   Lunges
❏   One-legged squats with raised rear leg
❏   One-legged climber forwards and sideways
❏   Squat with varying knee angles
❏   Ski position
❏   Leg press
❏   Jumps and landings forwards, backwards and sideways
❏   Step jumps, hops, specific imitation and regulation movements on one or two legs
❏   Leg curls (leg extension)

Exercises for Leg Flexion Musculature

❏   Leg flexion exercises supine position supported on the shoulders (on the floor, on a medicine ball, on the theraband)
❏   Leg flexion exercise standing up with theraband
❏   Leg flexion machine standing up
❏   Leg flexion machine prone position

Exercises for Lateral Leg Musculature (Adductors and Abductors)

- ❏ Lateral abduction outwards and inwards with ankle weights or with theraband
- ❏ Exercise on adductor and abductor machine
- ❏ Lateral imitation movements and jumps

Exercises for Trunk Musculature and for whole body tension

- ❏ Sit-ups: straight and diagonal
- ❏ Oblique ab exercises
- ❏ Abs exercise with straightened, raised legs, supine position
- ❏ Back exercises, prone position with varied arm positions
- ❏ Side exercises supported on elbow
- ❏ Forward push-ups
- ❏ Backward push-ups
- ❏ Side exercises, lying on trunk moving arms and legs up and down
- ❏ Back exercises: support on hands and feet with straightened legs, then varying arm positions supported on one or both feet
- ❏ Ab machines
- ❏ Prone position and standing back machines
- ❏ All kinds of cable pulley exercises, lateral and frontal
- ❏ Exercises with theraband, especially diagonal pulls

Exercises for the Upper Body, Arms and Shoulders

- ❏ Bench press
- ❏ Bench pull
- ❏ Lat pulls
- ❏ Neck press
- ❏ Dumbbell exercises
- ❏ Cable pulley exercises
- ❏ Push-ups
- ❏ Bicep curls
- ❏ Pull-ups
- ❏ Lateral arm raises with additional load

Strength Training Program

Selected strength training programs are set out below, along with in-depth explanations for every athlete. The programs are conceived, so that each one constitutes a training session. Most programs can also be combined with coordination training (e.g. balance training,...)

⇨ **Basic Strength training for several muscle groups without equipment or with light equipment**

Training goal, Explanations
❑   Improvement and development of general strength and general athletic ability
❑   Warm up with about 15 min. running or ergometer or light coordination exercises
❑   Warm down after session by stretching the muscles used for about 15 min.
❑   The training can be done without a weights room
❑   Light weights, Swiss balls, therabands, steps or low boxes can be used

Exercises, methods: the ski coach advises!
❑   Forwards and/or sideways lunges, 3 sets of 15 reps. on each side
❑   Bending exercises with one leg in shoulder support position backwards, 3 sets of 15 reps. on each side
❑   Straight sit-ups, 3 sets of 30 reps.
❑   Prone position back exercises with controlled up, down, sideways and rotational movements of the upper body and with varied arm positions, e.g. stretched out to the side for 1 minute, 3 sets
❑   Deep two-legged squats with a bar on the chest, 3 sets of 15 reps.
❑   Lateral exercises supported on the elbow (you can also raise and lower the upper leg), 3 sets of 30 seconds
❑   Forward push-ups, 3 sets of 20 reps.
❑   One legged bending and stretching in the ski position with eyes closed, 3 sets of 20 reps.
❑   Jumping from and into the ski position, with controlled landing, 3 sets of 10 reps.

Lunge

*Deep Squat with bar
held in front of chest*

Prone position back exercise

*Side exercise
with elbow support*

Comments

- ❏ The program is ideal for circuit training, or as a block (combination of 2-4 exercises).
- ❏ The rest should be from 30-90 seconds.
- ❏ The order of the exercises can be varied.
- ❏ Interacting muscle groups should be trained consecutively.
- ❏ The repetitions and load times should extend to muscle exhaustion.
- ❏ The movement speed is average, and regulative during both positive and negative muscle activity.
- ❏ The program is suitable for all target groups.

➡️ **Basic strength training for several muscle groups in the weight room**

Training Goal, Comments
- ❏   Improvement and development of general strength and general athletic ability, general muscle building training
- ❏   Warm up with about 15 min. running or ergometer and light coordination exercises
- ❏   Warm down by stretching the muscles used in training for about 15 minutes.
- ❏   Training can be carried out in a normally equipped weight room or fitness studio

Exercises, methods, the ski coach advises!
- ❏   Two-legged leg press with up to about 90° knee angle, additional weight 50-60%, 12-15 reps., 3-5 sets
- ❏   Leg flexion machine either lying or standing, one leg, additional weight about 50%, 12-15 reps., 3-5 sets
- ❏   Bench press with log bar, additional weight about 50%, 12-15 reps., 3-5 sets
- ❏   Pulley – diagonal pulls or with theraband, additional weight about 50%, 12-15 reps., 3-5 sets
- ❏   Straight sit-ups alternating with oblique sit-ups, 30-40 reps., 3-5 sets
- ❏   Back raises on the back extension machine with carrying arm position and regulated lateral and rotational movements, 30 reps., 3-5 sets
- ❏   One-legged lunges or squats with front leg on balance device and rear leg on boxes, additional load about 20-30%, bar on shoulders or carrying light weights in the hands, 12-15 reps., 3-5 sets.
- ❏   Lateral leg abduction outward and inward with additional weight about 30-50%. 12-15 reps., 3-5 sets.
- ❏   Ski position with eyes closed on balance device, 1 min., 3-5 sets
- ❏   Two-legged jumps with legs tucked up slightly to the side or over training hurdles, 10 reps., 3-5 sets

Comments
- ❏   The program can be carried out in block form (a combination of 2-4 exercises) or in classic form (consecutive exercises).

Diagonal theraband pulls

One legged squats with box

Leg abduction with theraband

Ski position on wobble board or ball

❏   Rest for 30 seconds to 2 minutes depending on the exercise.

❏   Rest can be active, with additional balancing exercises or concentration activities (e.g. ball juggling).

❏   The order of the exercises can be varied.

❏   Interacting muscle groups should be trained consecutively.

❏   The exercises should be carried out at average to fast speeds, and regulative movements both in the positive and negative muscle work phases.

❏   This program is suitable for all target groups.

▢⟩   **Special Basic Strength Training for the Trunk Musculature**

Training Goal/ Comments

❏   Improvement and development of general strength and general athletic ability, particularly in the trunk musculature
❏   Warm up with about 15 minutes running of ergometer and light coordination exercises
❏   Warm down by stretching the muscles used for about 15 minutes, or perform additional training, e.g. basic endurance session or a short coordination session.
❏   Training can be carried out without a weight room. The use of light weights, Swiss ball, balance devices and theraband makes training more effective.

Exercises, Methods, the ski coach advises!

❏   Ab exercises lying on the back with diagonal movements of the opposing arms and legs, 30 reps., 3-4 sets
❏   One-legged bottom extension backwards in shoulder support position. 12-15 reps. each side, 3-4 sets.
❏   Push ups, 30 reps., 3-4 sets
❏   Lateral exercises, lying on your side on the floor, lower leg is bent, upper leg straight with alternate up and down movements of the legs and trunk. 15 reps. each side, 3-4 sets.
❏   Carving exercise lying on your side supported by one arm with dynamic alternation, 10-12 reps. each side, 3-4 sets
❏   Whole body tension lying on side with only the hips touching the floor, legs closed and arms stretched beyond the head. Roll on your back from one side to the other. 5-6 reps., 3-4 sets
❏   Ab exercise lying on back with legs extended upwards and slightly apart, move the trunk up and down. Legs can also be supported on a Swiss ball. 20 reps., 3-4 sets
❏   Back exercise in standing position, regulated tensing of back muscles using theraband. Arms bent upwards and shoulders pulled back, 15-20 reps., 3-4 sets
❏   Diagonal trunk exercise standing on one and two legs. Pull the theraband diagonally across the front of the body. 15 reps. each side, 3-4 sets.

Comments

❏ The program can be carried out in block form (combination of 2-4 exercises) or in classic form (consecutive exercises).

❏ Recovery time is 30 seconds to 2 minutes, depending on the exercise.

❏ The order of the exercises can be varied.

❏ Interacting muscle groups should be trained consecutively.

❏ The reps. and load times should continue up to muscle exhaustion. This is essential for the desired training effect, especially for the trunk muscles.

❏ The spine should be neutral at all times (back is neither hollowed or rounded). An imaginary line should run between the head and the feet through the center of the body.

❏ Exercises should be carried out at an average to slow speed, both in the positive and negative muscle work phases.

❏ So-called core stability training is a vital foundation of strength training for ski sports. If it cannot be done as a separate training session due to the lack of time, a few of these exercises can be included in every training session as part of the warm-up.

❏ This program is suitable for all target groups.

Oblique ab exercise

Carving exercise

Back exercise standing on one leg

Ab exercise with Swiss ball and straight legs

Back exercise with theraband

⮕   **Special basic strength training for the leg musculature**

Training Goal, Comments

❏   Improvement and development of muscle efficiency, increased strength and muscle building of the ski-specific leg musculature (ski-specific basic strength).

❏   To warm up: about 15 minutes running or ergometer and light coordination exercises.

❏   10-15 minutes trunk strengthening exercises and 1-2 balance exercises.

❏   Warm down with 15 minutes stretching of the main muscles worked during the training session, or additional training such as basic endurance session or a short coordination training session.

❏   This training should be done in a weight room or fitness studio.

❏   The use of training aids such as balance devices or light weights make training more effective.

Exercises, Methods, the ski coach advises!

❏   Full squats with the bar on the shoulders or the chest, about 50% of max. load, 10-12 reps. or 20 seconds, 5 sets.

❏   One-legged leg curls, possibly also with static holds between the reps., 50-70% of max. load, 10-12 reps., or 20 seconds, 5 sets

❏   Series of star jumps, 10 reps., 5 sets

❏   One-legged leg press, knee angle up to 80°, possibly also with static holds between reps., 50-60% of max. load, 10-12 reps. or 20 seconds, 5 sets

❏   One-legged flexion exercises on the flexion machine, 50-70% of max. load, 10-12 reps. or 20 seconds, 5 sets

❏   Squats with different knee angles (sideways on step) with long or short bar, 50-60% of max. load, 10-12 reps. or 20 seconds, 5 sets

❏   Balancing exercise in ski position with imitation movements on balance device, 40 seconds – 1 minute, 5 sets

Full squats with weight

One-legged squats

Squats with varying knee angles

Comments

- ❑ The program can be carried out in block form (a combination of 2-4 exercises) or in classic form (consecutive exercises).
- ❑ Recovery time is about 2-3 minutes.
- ❑ The order of the exercises should not be changed.
- ❑ The reps. and load times should extend up to muscle exhaustion.
- ❑ The movement speed is average to very fast. Fast movement speed increases muscle efficiency; slow movement speed builds strength.
- ❑ Rock briefly 2 or 3 times during the exercise for variation.
- ❑ Pyramid training is very effective, e.g. with 8 – 10 – 12 – 10 – 8 reps.
- ❑ This program is suitable for all target groups.
- ❑ The basic leg program is essential for specific strength building of the leg musculature.
- ❑ Add a short upper body training session, part of a coordination training session, or a few speed exercises as a second training session.

⇨ Basic strength training for the upper body

Training goal, Comments
- ❑ Improvement and development of muscle efficiency, strength increase and muscle building of the upper body
- ❑ Warm up with about 15 minutes running or ergometer and light coordination exercises
- ❑ 10-15 minutes trunk strengthening exercises and 1 or 2 balance exercises
- ❑ Warm down by stretching the main muscles worked during the session for 15 minutes
- ❑ Training should be carried out in a weight room or a fitness studio
- ❑ Equipment like balance devices or small weights make training more effective

Exercises, Methods: the ski coach advises!
- ❑ Neck press with the long bar, 50-60% of max. load, 10-12 reps., 5 sets
- ❑ Bench press with long bar, 50-60% of max. load, 10-12 reps., 5 sets
- ❑ Lat pulls, 50-60%, 10-12 reps., 5 sets
- ❑ Sideways diagonal pulls on the pulley, or with a theraband, 50-60% of max. load, 10-12 reps., 5 sets
- ❑ Bench pulls with the long bar or dumbbells, 50-60% of max. load, 10-12 reps., 5 sets
- ❑ Pull-ups to the chest and the back of the neck, possibly with additional weight, e.g. ankle weights or made easier with the theraband. As many reps. as possible, 3 sets
- ❑ Under arm dips, possibly with feet raised and resting on a small box. As many reps. as possible.
- ❑ Push-ups on the floor, with the hands on a bar with weights and the feet on a Swiss ball, as many reps. as possible.

Comments
- ❑ The program can be carried out in block form (a combination of 2-4 exercises) or in classic form (consecutive exercises).

❏ Rest time about 2-3 minutes.

❏ Do not change the order of the exercises.

❏ The reps. and load times should extend until muscle exhaustion; do as many reps. as possible per set, then reduce the resistance so that reps. can be continued.

❏ The movement speed is average to very fast. Fast speed increases muscle efficiency, and slow speed builds strength.

❏ Pyramid training – with e.g. 8 – 10 – 12 – 10 – 8 reps. is very effective.

❏ This program is suitable for all target groups.

❏ The basic upper body program is essential for a specific strength increase in the upper body.

❏ This session is often performed after the above leg training session and also mainly with coordination training sessions.

Push-ups on weighted bar and Swiss ball

⇨ **Specific strength endurance training for the leg musculature, with Imitation exercises**

Training Goal, Comments
❏ Improvement and development of ski specific strength endurance for the leg musculature, with ski-specific coordination.
❏ Warm up with about 15 minutes running or ergometer, then a few trunk strengthening and balance exercises.
❏ The training program can be carried out with or without additional weights.

Exercises, Methods: the ski coach advises!
❏ A variety of squats up to a knee angle of about 90° (about 5 seconds static holds, then 6-8 reps., etc), about 30% of max. load, 45 seconds-2 minutes, 3-6 sets
❏ Two-legged leg press in series combined with static holds (hold for about 5 seconds, then 6-8 reps., etc.), about 30% of max. load, 45
❏ Ski position jumps up and downhill (in the mountains or on a sloping surface) 45 seconds-2 minutes, 3-6 sets
❏ Ski position simulation on balance device, 45 seconds-2 minutes, 3-6 sets
❏ Imitation jumps on two adjacent trampettes, sideways in the ski position, possibly rocking 2 or 3 times on the trampette 45-90 seconds, 3-6 sets
❏ Sideways jumps series over training hurdles about 20 cm high, 45 seconds-1 minute, 3-5 sets
❏ Side steps in low ski position backward and forward on a soft mat, 45-90 seconds, 3-5 sets
❏ Jumps circuit with boxes or similar obstacles, 45 seconds-1 minute, 3-5 sets

Comments
❏ The program can be carried out in the classic way, i.e. consecutive exercises. It can also be done as circuit training by shortening the load time.

❑ Do 3-8 minutes active recovery, e.g. light bike ergometer riding or loose movements

❑ Do not change the order of the exercises.

❑ Reps. and load times should go right to muscle exhaustion.

❑ Strength endurance training is very demanding in terms of will power and motivation.

❑ Movements are carried out at ski-specific speed.

❑ This program is suitable for all target groups.

❑ The exercises should be carried out without additional weights in the case of young school-age and junior athletes.

*Simulated Inclined
Ski Position*

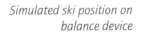

*Simulated ski position on
balance device*

⇨   **Specific speed strength training for leg musculature**

Training Goal, Comments
❑   Improvement and development of ski-specific leg speed-strength, combined with ski-specific coordination.
❑   Warm up with about 15 minutes running or games, a few trunk strengthening, gymnastic and coordination exercises, e.g. jumps.
❑   Warm down after the session with a short gymnastic program or jog.
❑   The training program contains exercises with and without additional load and can therefore be done in the open air, in the gym or in the weight room.
❑   Include no more than 3-5 of the above-mentioned exercises in each training session.

Exercises, Methods: the ski coach advises!
❑   Two-legged leg press, moving legs as fast as possible, 30-50 % of max. load, 6-8 reps., 4-5 sets
❑   Two-legged reactive jumps forwards or sideways, e.g. over hurdles, 6-8 reps., 4-5 sets
❑   Squats with bar or with small weights, 30-50 % of max. load, 6-8 reps., 4-5 sets
❑   Jumps from ski position, e.g. jumping off box. 6-8 reps., 4-5 sets
❑   Reactive wobbling in the ski position on the trampette or on a wobble board, about 10-12 seconds, 4-5 sets
❑   One-legged squats with the bar or with small weights, about 30-50 % max. load. 4-5 reps. each side, 4-5 sets
❑   Foot tapping, i.e. fast feet in the ski position. About 10-12 seconds, 4-5 sets
❑   Movement combinations, e.g. jumps circuit, combination of runs and jumps, about 10- 20 seconds, 4-5 sets

Comments
❑   The above exercises can either be carried out one after the other, or in a circuit by shortening the load time.

- ❏ Allow for 5 minutes active recovery.
- ❏ Do not change the order of the exercises.
- ❏ After an exercise with additional load, do a coordination speed-strength exercise.
- ❏ Speed-strength training is very demanding in terms of concentration and movement motor function.
- ❏ Movement speed is 100%; aim for a short ground contact time in the jumps; in all exercises aim for an explosive movement, transfer between flexion and extension.
- ❏ This program is suitable for all target groups.
- ❏ Young school-age and junior athletes should perform these exercises without additional load.
- ❏ Speed-strength training can only be effective if the athlete's basic strength and motor skills are already relatively well developed.
- ❏ Avoid speed-strength training in the case of fatigue or slight injury.

One-legged squat with bar

The above program can be complemented with other effective ways of developing strength ability as follows:

Mountain jogging
- Strength endurance for the legs

Mountain Bike riding uphill + cross country
- Strength endurance, leg speed-strength

Mountain Bike Interval Training
- Strength endurance, leg speed-strength

Specific cycling strength program, e.g. 5 x 1 min. highly intensive riding in high gear, time trial training, mountain training
- Strength endurance and maximal leg strength

Athletics jumps
- Speed-strength and motor skills

Gymnastics and competitive sports
- Whole body strength, coordination and balance

Inline skating, Cross country skiing, e.g. uphill intervals
- Strength endurance, leg speed strength

Coordination/Speed Program

The demand profile for alpine skiing shows that it is one of the most difficult sports in terms of movement technique and specific motor skills. This explains why quite specific speed ability is necessary to create better physical preconditions for easier learning and a complete transfer of the ski technique. The ability to adapt to different situations is vitally important here. This means that demands on the movement technique can differ greatly according to, e.g. snow type, slope condition, slope profile, weather and light conditions, etc., and this must be taken into account and prepared for in training from summer onwards. Compared to classic speed sports, like the sprints and jumps in athletics, or classic composition sports like Olympic Gymnastics, the speed and coordination components of ski sports are difficult to separate and should, in fact, be dealt with and trained together. There are many ways of training these ski specifics in conditioning training already. General and partly specific coordination and speed training should begin at age six, when the first talents emerge in the clubs, and continue right up to the highest performance levels. Alpine speed skiers are renowned for having very well developed coordination and all-round athleticism.

Exercises and Methods for Special Coordination and Speed Training

The classic method for speed and motor skills training is the repetition or interval method. The repetitions of an exercise vary greatly according to their difficulty and the load time. In general, load times are short, 6-30 seconds, and longer for very complex exercises. Recovery is short to average (30 seconds-3 minutes, and longer for extremely complex exercises). The aim is to develop the movement quality to the highest level of variable availability, and to master as many movements as possible. The intensity often depends on the quality of the movement. For effective training, the movement speed s and energy input should be very intensive and specific to the exercise. Maximal input in this case does not mean optimal input. At the elite level, there are also methods in which coordination elements are combined with strength training.

The training is mainly done in block form (several exercises in a block), and circuit training is also very common. Those who train alone should note that coordination and speed training elements require constant correction, improving and analyzing, which means that group training, e.g. in a club or gym is really useful. The most important thing is the choice of exercise and the intention behind it. Below we present a selection of the most important exercises intended for different aspects of speed and coordination training for ski sports. It includes general and also very specific exercises. Part of the exercises can be carried out with no equipment; many require equipment such as hurdles, markers, boxes, trampolines, mats, special training equipment, etc.

The illustration below shows the connection between general and specific coordination and ski technique.

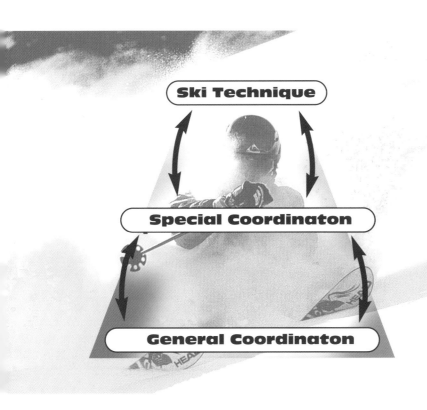

Exercises for General Speed and Coordination

- ❏ All athletic running drills, e.g. skipping, foot tapping, high knees running, heel walking, crossovers, sidesteps, ankling, sprinting, runs with change of direction, hop running etc...
- ❏ All general jumping drills e.g. two-legged jumps, one-legged jumps, hurdle jumps, stride change jumps, sideways jumps, backward jumps, rhythm jumps, etc...
- ❏ All basic gymnastic exercise e.g. rolls, cartwheel, handstand, supports, holds, hanging, swings, etc..
- ❏ Many games and sports, e.g. ball games, hockey, tennis, inline skating...

Exercises for Specific Balancing Ability

- ❏ Balancing forward, backward, sideways on beams, poles, ropes, special equipment
- ❏ Ski-typical movements on balance devices, e.g. wobble boards, balls, etc...
- ❏ Specific training with inline skates and snowshoes, all kinds of take-offs and landings...

Exercises for Specific-complex Movement Motor Skills

- ❏ Changes of direction combined with running, jumps and obstacle courses
- ❏ Exercises on different surfaces, e.g. jumps circuits with boxes, trampettes, mats
- ❏ Speed circuit with training hurdles and cones (combining e.g. slalom runs, jumps, sprints, gymnastic exercises)
- ❏ Perception and reaction exercises, exercises for visual reactions, concentration exercises

Exercises for Specific Speed Abilities

- ❏ All kinds of cadence "fast feet" drills combined with ski-typical movements
- ❏ Imitation exercises and jumps, e.g. sideways jumps, step jumps, one-legged jumps, ski position imitations with fast feet, speed drills on different surfaces (trampettes, boards, mats)

Training Program for Specific Coordination and Speed in Ski Sports

Effective training is guaranteed when the exercises and methods are adapted to the training goal. In the following pages, we present specific selected programs, and give detailed explanations as to how to implement them. Experience shows that to improve performance, it helps to follow a training program, but also to adapt training according to circumstances.

Both athlete and coach should try to make a healthy evaluation of the situation to master the tightrope walk between a sensible reduction of the training workload (obvious tiredness, aches and pains, significant lack of motivation...) and "self-deception". After all, training is a personal thing!

The programs are conceived so that only selected parts should be carried out in each training session, as the actual movement level and movement quality are very important particularly in terms of coordination. Normally, in a coordination session the contents are combined. So for example, the first part consists of complex-motor training, the second part of a balancing section. If training is limited to certain contents only, the result is a blocking of motor skills and resulting imbalances.

As an all-around movement repertoire facilitates the learning of new, complex tasks, it is worth making coordination training as comprehensive as possible at school age and youth level. In competitive sports, certain coordination sessions are also combined with strength sessions (e.g. balance training...).

Specific balance training

Training Goal, Comments
- ❑ Improve and develop ski-specific balance regulation.
- ❑ Warm up with about 15 minutes running, or general coordination exercises, and games together with a few trunk strengthening exercises.
- ❑ Warm down with about 15 minutes stretching of the main muscle groups exercised, or do another training session, e.g. endurance or strength training.
- ❑ Balance equipment (beams, poles, rope) and balance device (wobble board, pivot board, balls...) can be used for certain exercises.

Exercises, methods: the ski coach advises!
- ❑ Balancing forward and backward on a tightrope, beam or pole, possibly also while bending down and stretching up. 30 seconds-1 minute, 3-5 attempts
- ❑ Balancing sideways on a tightrope, beam or pole, possibly also while bending down and stretching up. 30 seconds-1 minute, 3-5 attempts
- ❑ Sideways jump followed by balancing in the ski position, about 10 seconds, 5-8 attempts
- ❑ Standing on a balance device (wobble board, propriotrainer, pivot board, etc) in different positions on two legs and one leg, 30 seconds-1 minute, 5 attempts
- ❑ Standing on one leg and trying to keep balance in the basic ski positions with the eyes closed. 30 seconds-1 minute, 3-5 attempts
- ❑ One-legged squats with a knee angle of up to 90° on balance device (wobble board, propriotrainer, pivot board, etc...) 30 seconds-1 minute, 3-5 attempts
- ❑ Jumps series on trampette, possibly with more than one trampette, 30 seconds-1 minute, 3-5 attempts
- ❑ Sitting, kneeling and standing on Swiss ball and trying to balance, 5 attempts or more
- ❑ Circuit of different balance exercises one after the other (increasing in difficulty)
- ❑ Learning to ride a pedalo and a monocycle

Comments

❏ The program is ideal for a circuit training format or a block training (combination of 2-4 exercises) format.

❏ Difficult exercises should be repeated frequently.

❏ The rest time should be 30-90 seconds; the exercises are always tackled when you are 100 % concentrated.

❏ The order of the exercises can be varied.

❏ It is absolutely vital to master the exercises, and to perform them with optimal movement technique.

❏ The target groups include beginners, and also more experienced athletes and competitive skiers, particularly school age and junior up and coming athletes.

*Standing on
the Swiss ball*

⇨ Ski-specific complex movement motor skills

Training Goal, Comments

❑ Improve and develop ski-specific-complex movement motor skills.

❑ Improve adaptation and conversion ability, orientation ability, imitating ski movements, and rhythmic ability.

❑ Warm up with about 15 minutes running, or general coordination exercises and games combined with a few trunk strengthening exercises.

❑ Warm down with about 15 minutes stretching of the main muscle groups used or carry out another training session, e.g. endurance or strength training.

❑ Gymnastics apparatus, training hurdles, cones and mats are all useful training aids. Training can also be done in the open air using natural features as equipment for exercises.

Exercises, methods: the ski coach advises!

❑ Side steps with typical ski movements (ski position, basic positions) and additional tasks, such as ball throwing, 30 seconds, 3 attempts

❑ Imitation jumps sideways over 20cm high hurdles, 8 reps., then roll forward and backward, then specific two-legged jumps forward and sideways, 8 reps., 3 attempts

❑ Running and jumping circuits with runs using natural features, e.g. steep downhill, over trees, under fences, etc. About 30 seconds, 3 attempts

❑ Combination of strengthening exercises, e.g. squats, followed by imitation circuit, 6 – 8 reps. squats followed by 20 seconds imitation circuit. 3 attempts

❑ Ski movements (bending, stretching on sloping surfaces with knees bent at different angles to the left and right or ski position with and without poles) with the eyes closed. 30 seconds – 1 minute, 3 – 5 attempts

❑ Rhythmic running and jumping combinations, e.g. 4 x fast hopping run, 6 slow, controlled leg change jumps, 12 two-legged jumps with intermediate skips on command, fast sidesteps to and fro, can be done as a synchronized partner exercise

Comments

- ❏ The program is ideal for a circuit training format or a block training format (combination of 2-4 exercises).
- ❏ The rest periods should be from 30 to 90 seconds, so that the exercises can be done with 100 % concentration.
- ❏ The order of the exercises can be varied.
- ❏ It is absolutely vital to master the exercises, and to perform them with optimal movement technique.
- ❏ The better an athlete is, the more complex an exercise can be.
- ❏ The target groups include beginners, and also more experienced athletes and competitive skiers, particularly school age and junior up and coming athletes.

*Ski imitation exercise
on sloping surface*

⇨ Ski-specific speed program

Training Goal, Explanations
- ❑ Improve and develop ski-specific forms of speed.
- ❑ Perform complex movements as fast as possible and achieve high elementary speed abilities (frequency).
- ❑ Warm up with about 15 minutes running or general coordination exercises and games combined with a few trunk strengthening exercises, acceleration runs, jumps or short sprints.
- ❑ Warm down with about 15 minutes stretching of the main muscle groups used or carry out another training session, e.g. endurance or strength training.
- ❑ Gymnastics apparatus, training hurdles, cones and mats are useful training aids. Training can also take place in the open air using natural features.

Exercises, Methods: the ski coach advises!
- ❑ "Fast feet" left and right in place, about 8 seconds, 3-5 attempts
- ❑ "Fast feet" left and right in the ski position, about 8 seconds, 3-5 attempts
- ❑ Sidesteps about 3 minutes, to and fro, while adopting various typical ski positions, about 10-15 seconds, 3-5 attempts
- ❑ Reaction movements, sprints or jumps, possibly with additional tasks involving changing movement direction on visual signals (can also be done as a partner exercise) 3-5 seconds, 3-5 attempts
- ❑ Speed circuit with cones and movement combinations, e.g. sprints to cones, sidesteps to the next cone, sprint backward to the next cone, sidesteps to the next cone, sprint forward to the next cone max. of about 8, 15 seconds, 3-5 attempts
- ❑ Speed and/or jumps circuit combined with simple gymnastic elements (e.g. forward roll, then backward roll, then 4 jumps over hurdles, then 8 sideways, jumps over cones to and fro, then forward sprint, about 8-15 seconds, 3-5 attempts
- ❑ "Fast feet" with left and right feet on different surfaces (soft mats, trampette, springboard), about 6-8 seconds, 3-5 attempts

❏ Open air speed circuit with sprints, jumps, imitation exercises, e.g. using steps or mountain paths with varying terrain, about 8-15 seconds, 3-5 attempts

Comments

❏ The program is ideal for a circuit training format or a block training format (combination of 2-4 exercises).

❏ Do not include more than 3-5 exercises in any one training session.

❏ Part of the program can also be integrated into a strength session or combined with balance exercises or motor skills exercises.

❏ Difficult exercises should be repeated more frequently.

❏ Rests should last 1-2 minutes, so that the exercises are always done with 100% concentration.

❏ The training volume depends on "speed fatigue", i.e. the exercises should be made easier or stopped altogether once the initial movement, speed, or frequency cannot be maintained.

❏ The order of the exercises can be varied.

❏ It is absolutely vital to master the exercises, and to perform them with optimal movement technique.

❏ The better an athlete is, the more complex an exercise can be.

❏ The target groups include beginners, and also more experienced athletes and competitive skiers, particularly school age and junior up and coming athletes, and athletes in rehabilitation.

As well as the previously mentioned programs, the following activities are also effective ways of developing coordination and speed.

▷ **Inline skating emphasizing ski technique, keeping balance, half pipe...**
 ❏   Specific motor skills

▷ **Climbing, high rope course**
 ❏   Keeping balance, overcoming fear and concentration

▷ **Waterskiing, surfing, windsurfing, skateboarding**
 ❏   Keeping balance, concentration, overcoming fear

▷ **Mountain Bike, trail riding**
 ❏   Keeping balance, concentration, overcoming fear

▷ **Inline hockey, ice hockey**
 ❏   Keeping balance, speed

▷ **Cross-country skiing, skating, snowboarding**
 ❏   Keeping balance, specific motor skills

Endurance Training Program

As you can see in the demand profile, the specific endurance form of strength endurance is very important, particularly for the legs. Basic endurance should not be neglected either as good basic endurance is essential for quick recovery between sessions to enable the required number of training sessions per week for both modern recreational and competitive training to be carried out.

As ski sports are often practiced at altitudes of over 2000m, good basic endurance is required to be able to sustain the ski technique and to continue to enjoy the sport. Without endurance, limits are reached very quickly and fatigue can seriously limit the learning process. It is also annoying not to be able to really take advantage of deep snow on a fantastic free riding day.

There are a variety of ways of developing basic and specific, sometimes highly intensive specific, endurance. Running, mountaineering and hiking, hill running and trial running, road cycling, mountain biking on mountain roads, paths and trails, and as cross-country training in difficult terrains, inline skating, Nordic walking and classic cross-country skiing, as well as skating, bike ergometer, spinning, treadmill running in indoor training facilities complete the range of training possibilities.

Endurance Training Content

Below we have summarized different types of endurance training, and their effectiveness, and training effect for ski sports.

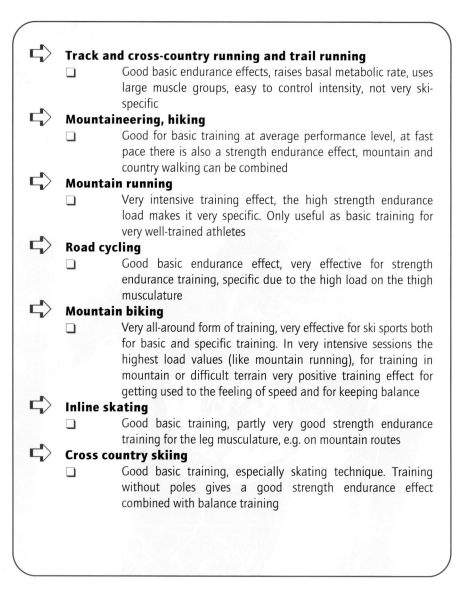

Track and cross-country running and trail running
❑   Good basic endurance effects, raises basal metabolic rate, uses large muscle groups, easy to control intensity, not very ski-specific

Mountaineering, hiking
❑   Good for basic training at average performance level, at fast pace there is also a strength endurance effect, mountain and country walking can be combined

Mountain running
❑   Very intensive training effect, the high strength endurance load makes it very specific. Only useful as basic training for very well-trained athletes

Road cycling
❑   Good basic endurance effect, very effective for strength endurance training, specific due to the high load on the thigh musculature

Mountain biking
❑   Very all-around form of training, very effective for ski sports both for basic and specific training. In very intensive sessions the highest load values (like mountain running), for training in mountain or difficult terrain very positive training effect for getting used to the feeling of speed and for keeping balance

Inline skating
❑   Good basic training, partly very good strength endurance training for the leg musculature, e.g. on mountain routes

Cross country skiing
❑   Good basic training, especially skating technique. Training without poles gives a good strength endurance effect combined with balance training

Endurance Training Methods

In endurance training for ski sports, the training goals are determined both by the training contents and the training methods used. In endurance training, the load is a product of the combination of intensity (running speed, cycling speed, power input, stride length and stride frequency) with the indirect load parameters like heart rate, or the type of energy production system. There are two basic types of energy production systems:

⇨ Sufficient oxygen supply in the muscles (aerobic energy production)

⇨ Energy production without sufficient oxygen (anaerobic energy production)

In addition, the training volume (length of training session, training distance, altitude and mileage) also determines the load.

The training methods are also derived from the training areas that are most important for training practice. On the following page, we set out the most important training areas for ski sports.

TRAINING ZONES

Training Zone	Abbreviation	Short Description
Recovery/Compensation zone	Rec/Com	Lowest intensity (heart rate about 120 bpm) low volume (60 minutes at the most), recovery training
Basic zone	BZ	Basic endurance training, low to average intensity (HR to about 150 bpm), high volume (up to several hours), mainly fat metabolism and aerobic energy production, light to average effort
Development zone	DZ	Average to high intensity (HR up to about 170 bpm), average volume (1-2 hours) and interval loading, fat and carbohydrate metabolism, high energy input, training in aerobic/anaerobic threshold zone, average to high effort
Elite zone	EZ	High to highest intensity (HR up to maximal bpm), low volume (30 minutes), mainly interval form with average load times, or can also be done as endurance competition training, anaerobic carbohydrate metabolism, high energy input, high to highest effort
Strength and Speed Strength zone	SS	Average to high intensity and highest and fastest possible energy input, low volume, only possible in interval form with short load times, special strength characteristic combined with endurance sports, anaerobic phosphate metabolism, high, short effort
Strength endurance zone	SE	High to highest intensity (HR up to maximal bpm), high strength level for long periods, low to average volume, usually in interval form, high to highest effort

The most important endurance training methods for ski sports arise from the training zones.

Endurance Methods

ENDURANCE METHODS		
Zone	Length	Intensity
BZ	45 min.-several hours	HR about 130-150 bpm
DZ	30 min.-about 2 hours	HR about 150-170 bpm
EZ	Up to about 30 min.	HR about 180-maximal bpm

Training Structure
The continuous endurance method is most commonly used. For ski sports training, it is a very good idea to combine different zones within one training session (variable endurance method), e.g. due to varied and mountainous terrain covered. However, if you stick to one type of terrain, it is easier to stick to one training zone.

Implementation/Explanations
The endurance method is the most commonly used to improve endurance ability. Along with the intrinsic training effects, athletes also appreciate the experience of nature, and the mental side (will, motivation, feeling of flow).

The running load takes up the least possible training volume from the given load times and intensities, but the pulse rate is about 10 bpm higher than for cycling. In road cycling, mountain biking, and mountain running and climbing, very high intensities and volumes are possible; endurance training for ski sports should, therefore, always be combined with these sports. Training can start to be very varied if you combine types of sport in one training session (e.g. mountain biking then mountain climbing). The endurance method can be used by athletes of all ages and abilities. Specific endurance training should only be done when wearing a heart rate monitor.

Strength Endurance/Interval Methods

STRENGTH ENDURANCE/INTERVAL METHODS				
Zone	Duration	Number	Rest	Intensity
EZ – Interval	30 seconds -5 min.	3-8	3-20 minutes	HR up to max.
S and SS Interval	Up to 10 seconds	About 10	About 3 minutes	HR up to about 170 bpm
SE interval	1 min-about 30 min.	1-8	5-20 min.	HR up to max. bpm

Training Structure

The more intensive the load, the shorter the interval times should be. Interval training can also be included in an endurance session to make it more ski sport specific. It is very effective to include a speed strength interval session (e.g. 5 x 6 seconds) in a mountain bike training session, and to include strength endurance intervals in the longest uphill climbs.

Strength endurance, speed strength, and maximal strength intervals, in particular lend themselves very well to cycling or mountain biking. The rest structure depends on the loading, and also on how you feel.

Implementation/ Explanations

The interval methods are very important in ski sports specific endurance training. By varying the type of sport and terrain, training for the leg musculature can be made very specific. The interval method is most suitable for competition level athletes, but with adaptation (reduction of intensity), it can also be used very effectively by young school age athletes and by recreational athletes.

Endurance Training Program/Content

⇨ **General Basic Endurance Content**

Training Goal, Explanations
- ❑ Improve and develop general basic endurance.
- ❑ According to the discipline, warm up with 10 minutes of motor skills exercises, coordination or technique exercises (high stride rate, coordination runs, etc...). If necessary, and depending on how you feel, briefly stretch the main muscles you are going to work on and do 2 or 3 trunk strengthening exercises.
- ❑ To warm down, spend about 15 minutes stretching the main muscles used, or do another training session, e.g. core stability, upper body strength training.

Exercises, Methods: the ski coach advises!
- ❑ Running at different speeds between basic endurance and development endurance zones over varying terrain. 45-90 minutes, HR 140-170 bpm
- ❑ Mountain biking, cycling at varying speeds between basic and development endurance zones over varying terrain. 2-4 hours, HR 130-160 bpm
- ❑ Combined session of running and mountain bike/cycling basic endurance and development endurance over varying terrain. 90 minutes-2 hours, HR 140-175 bpm
- ❑ Mountain bike/cycling in the mountains, development zone with strength endurance intervals (according to the length of the hills) 1-2 hours, HR about 150-190 bpm
- ❑ Inline skating at varying speeds, basic, development and elite endurance, about 60 minutes, HR 140-190 bpm
- ❑ Mountain running, trail running, development zone with strength endurance intervals (short sprints and jumps). About 30 minutes-1 hour, HR 150-190 bpm

Comments
- ❑ We have deliberately presented many alternatives for basic endurance training, but only use one of each per training session.
- ❑ Always aim for optimal movement technique.

❑ In particular, the endurance sessions, like trail running, mountain biking, and inline skating are intended to integrate certain coordination elements, and to learn an awareness of and feeling for speed, and the need to adapt movements to varying situations.

❑ Regular and varied contact with the elements and nature in the mountains is also beneficial.

❑ This training is suitable for athletes of all ages and abilities; training for young athletes should be very varied.

➡️ **Specific strength endurance content and interval content for specific endurance**

Training Goal, Explanations

❑ Improve and develop specific strength endurance and specific endurance. According to discipline, warm up with 20 minutes circuit training in the sport concerned and do a few short sprints.

❑ Warm down with about 30 min. loose walking, jogging, etc., as well as stretching exercises.

Exercises, Methods: the ski coach advises!

❑ Running, cycling, mountain biking, inline skating elite level intervals, 3-5 x about 1 minute, HR up to 190 bpm, 5 minute rest

❑ Running, cycling, mountain biking, inline skating Development zone/elite zone intervals, 5-8 x about 3 minutes, HR up to 180 bpm, 10 minutes rest

❑ Mountain running, mountain biking, inline skating, skating in the mountains, strength endurance intervals, 3-5 x about 3-5 minutes, HR up to max. bpm, about 10-15 min. rest.

❑ Cross country mountain biking and trial running. Intervals on cross-country circuit or in the mountains with change of disciplines, 3-5 x 1-3 minutes, HR up to maximal bpm, about 10-15 minutes rest

Comments

❑ We have deliberately presented many alternative forms of basic endurance training; only one should be used in each training session though.

- ❑ Always ensure optimal movement technique.
- ❑ The endurance sessions, like trail running, mountain biking and inline skating, in particular are intended to incorporate certain coordination elements, and to learn an awareness of and feeling for speed, and the need to adapt movements to varying situations.
- ❑ Regular and varied contact with the elements and nature in the mountains is also beneficial.
- ❑ This training is suitable for athletes of all ages and abilities; training for young athletes should be very varied.

Flexibility Training Program

In ski sports, there is no special need for flexibility in any muscle groups, or for special amplitude of the joints. But muscles that are not shortened and a functional musculo-skeletal system are both absolutely essential for mastering the modern ski technique, and also good for injury prevention.

A skier should not only be strong and well coordinated, but also very functional. Good mobility of the hip joints and the spine are important. The functional development and maintenance of flexibility combined with core stability training is also necessary. The modern carving technique has increased the flexibility demands on the skier.

Wellness trends like yoga, holistic mind, body and spirit exercise, and Aiglesreiter training are particularly aimed at most people's lack of flexibility, including some top athletes. There are, consequently, many different ways of flexibility training for ski sports. Classic exercises, but also special exercises, especially for the leg musculature and hip flexibility, are very useful. Along with the intrinsic training effect, the improvement and the maintenance of flexibility, a stretching and flexibility program enables rapid recovery from and compensation for hard training and is vital for a holistic, positive body feeling.

Exercises to maintain and improve flexibility should be an integral part of the daily ski sports training. Flexibility training should begin with the most important exercises from late childhood on (from age 10), and continue for as long as sports are practiced.

Flexibility Training Methods

There are numerous ways of improving the flexibility and stretchability of muscles. The main difference between them lies in the type of muscle activity and in the hold time. In addition, there is another possibility, with additional tensing and relaxing of the muscles, to heighten the stretching effect.

The dynamic stretching method is better suited to preparing the muscles for training; the classic stretching and the yoga method, with very long hold times are better suited to improving flexibility and accelerating recovery. The following overview shows the most effective methods for flexibility training in sport.

STRETCHING METHODS		
Stretching Method	Load time	Training structure/ Implementation
Static stretching (classic stretching method)	30 seconds-1 minute, 1-3 attempts per exercise	For all ability levels, mainly after training, for fast movements, not as a warm-up
Static stretching (short stretching method)	4-max. 10 second stretches, 1-3 attempts per exercise	More suitable for experienced athletes, positive training effect before speed training or intensive strength training, muscular feeling
Brief, dynamic stretching with a little amplitude	2-3 times rocking in the starting position, 1-3 attempts per exercise	More suitable for experienced athletes, positive training effect before speed training of intensive strength training, muscular feeling
Stretching method with muscular contraction (Proprioceptive neuromuscular facilitation – PNF)	In the stretch position, 4-6 seconds of long maximal contraction of the muscle to be stretched, followed by a 30 second-1 minute stretch, 1-3 attempts	Very rapid training effect in the case of very poor flexibility, also useful in build-up training after injury, muscular feeling should be present
Yoga method	1-5 minutes, 1-2 attempts	Very effective for long-term improvement in flexibility, more suitable for experienced athletes

Below, we summarize the most important specific flexibility exercises. Other exercises for all muscle groups, as used for many sports, are naturally also recommended for ski sports.

Exercises, Methods: the ski coach advises!

❑   Make sure all exercises are performed correctly.
❑   In all exercises, keep a neutral spine, so that the pelvis does not tilt forward or backward, and keep the arms and legs in line with the body with the head up.

Supine position leg stretch

Kneeling quadriceps stretch

Standing hip and bottom stretch

Lying hip and bottom stretch

Hurdle sitting position

Two-legged butterfly stretch

Box splits

Splits with a straight back

One-sided lying back stretch

Squat

Calf stretch

VI EXAMPLES OF TRAINING CONCEPTS

T his final chapter contains a few examples of training concepts for use in conditioning preparation for ski sports corresponding to age and performance level. There are two training concepts for the youth level and one training concept for the performance-oriented fitness training for adults.

TRAINING PROGRAM

Ski Sports Conditioning training for 9 - 12 year-olds

Goals: Achieving high general conditioning and motor skills, introduction to special skills, achieving very good and completely all-around fitness, enjoyment of regular training

The ski coach advises: Children find competitions in training very motivating; make sure they are well organized with not too many explanations. Try to make the exercises very challenging.

June, July

Training contents
- [ ] General coordination (running – jumping – games)
- [ ] Basic trunk strengthening and general athletic training
- [ ] Basic flexibility exercises
- [ ] Simple elementary speed
- [ ] **Recreational endurance and outdoor sports, possibly in the form of competitions**
- [ ] Alternative sports (climbing, inline skating...)
- [ ] General summer sports (games, tennis, gymnastics, ballet, athletics...)

Training structure
- [ ] Conduct ski conditioning training twice weekly for about 90 min.
- [ ] Make the content of the training sessions mixed.
- [ ] Learn how to do exercises.
- [ ] Training sessions should take place mainly in the open air.
- [ ] Develop training motivation.

September, October, November

Training Contents:
- ❏ Special motor skills training (balance, specific movements, coordination paths)
- ❏ Complex speed circuit
- ❏ Endurance and outdoor sports
- ❏ Basic trunk strengthening and general athletic training
- ❏ Basic exercises for flexibility
- ❏ Strength-circuit training combined with coordination without additional weights (jumps, leg exercises, etc...)
- ❏ Incorporate conditioning competitions

Training Structure:
- ❏ Conduct ski conditioning training twice weekly for about 90 min., possibly add a third training session.
- ❏ Make the training sessions contents mixed.
- ❏ Develop training motivation and self-conquest.
- ❏ Consolidate exercises.
- ❏ Make training volume and contents appropriate for ski training.

December - April

Training Contents:
- ❏ General coordination and speed
- ❏ Special motor skills training (balance, specific movements, coordination paths)
- ❏ Basic trunk strengthening and general athletic training
- ❏ Other sports (ice hockey, ball games, cross country skating...)

Training Structure:
- ❏ Once weekly conduct ski conditioning training appropriate for ski training
- ❏ Vary conditioning training.
- ❏ Further develop general fitness.
- ❏ Conduct ski training in ski center three times weekly.

Ski Sports Conditioning training for 13 – 15 year-old competitive athletes

Goals:

Achieving high general conditioning and motor skills, developing of special skills, achieving of very good and completely all-around fitness, achieving motivation, will power.

The ski coach advises:

In this age group, compensate for weaknesses in the conditioning zone. Special functional strength and flexibility training for young people is very important; incorporate competitions and will-power training.

May, June, July

Training Contents:

- ❑ General coordination (running – jumping – games)
- ❑ Basic trunk strengthening and general athletic training
- ❑ Basic strength training with bodyweight only
- ❑ Basic flexibility exercises
- ❑ Simple endurance and outdoor sports with competitions
- ❑ Alternative sports (climbing, inline skating...)
- ❑ Practice other sports (games, tennis, gymnastics, athletics...)
- ❑ Tests for strengths and weaknesses

Training structure:

- ❑ Conduct ski conditioning training 2-3 x weekly for about 90 minutes.
- ❑ Make the training session contents mixed.
- ❑ Optimize exercises.
- ❑ Training sessions should take place mainly in the open air.
- ❑ Develop training motivation.

September, October, November

Training Contents:

- ❏ Special motor skills training (balance, specific movements, coordination paths)
- ❏ More complex speed circuit
- ❏ Practice endurance and outdoor sports
- ❏ Basic trunk strengthening and general athletic training
- ❏ Basic exercises for flexibility
- ❏ Strength circuit training combined with coordination without additional load (jumps, leg exercises, etc...)
- ❏ Strength endurance training legs
- ❏ Conditioning tests and competitions
- ❏ Testing for strengths and weaknesses

Training structure:

- ❏ Conduct ski conditioning training 3 times weekly for about 90 minutes, possibly add another training session.
- ❏ Conduct training sessions with focal points.
- ❏ Develop training will power and self-conquest.
- ❏ Vary exercises and make them more difficult.
- ❏ Adapt training volume and content to ski training.

December - April

Training Content:

- ❏ General coordination and speed
- ❏ Special motor skills training (balance, specific movement, coordination paths)
- ❏ Basic trunk strengthening and general athletic training
- ❏ Other sports (ice hockey, ball games, cross-country skating...)

Training Structure

- ❏ Conduct ski conditioning training 1 x a week appropriate for ski training.
- ❏ Vary conditioning training.
- ❏ Develop further general basic fitness.
- ❏ Develop further specific motor skills.
- ❏ Conduct 4-6 x weekly ski training in training centers with competitions.

Conditioning training for adult recreational skiers

Training Goals: Good general functional fitness, training of special abilities, work on conditioning weaknesses, enjoyment of developing all-around/holistic ski fitness for the coming skiing season

The ski coach advises: The emphasis is on holistic/all-around fitness; group training is very beneficial. Pay attention to physical condition.

May, June, July

Training Content:
- ❑ practice recreational endurance and outdoor sports
- ❑ try out new, alternative sports (climbing, inline skating...).
- ❑ Practice general summer sports (games, tennis...)
- ❑ Basic trunk strengthening and flexibility training
- ❑ Basic strength training for all muscle groups
- ❑ Summer sport competitions
- ❑ Possible endurance block with fitness vacation

Training Structure:
- ❑ Conduct general conditioning training for the relevant sport 2-4 x weekly
- ❑ Training sessions should have a focal point.
- ❑ Develop training motivation.

September, October, November

Training Contents:
- ❑ Special motor skills training (balance, specific movements)
- ❑ General strength training
- ❑ Specific strength and strength endurance training
- ❑ Alternative and outdoor sports
- ❑ Intensive core stability and flexibility training
- ❑ Medical check-up, possible endurance and strength performance tests

Training Structure:
- ❑ Conduct ski sports conditioning training combined with additional general training sessions 1-2 x a week.

December - April

Training Contents:
- ❑ Complimentary training with other sports
- ❑ General strength training
- ❑ Intensive core stability and flexibility training

Training Structure:
- ❑ Conduct training according to skiing frequency. Include at least one ski sport conditioning session per week.

Appendix

Photo Credits

Internal photos: **HEAD Ski:** Pages 3, 5 (from the top: 1, 2, 5 and 6), 8, 10, 18, 22, 24, 28/29, 32, 42, 45, 52, 56, 63, 66, 73, 76, 78, 80, 86, 89, 93, 100
XnX GmbH: Pages 5 (from the top: 3 and 4), 16, 17, 23, 30, 41, 44, 48, 49, 51, 57, 59, 68, 70, 88, 90, 91, 112
Gerwig Löffelholz: pages 6, 7
Ralf Schäuble: Pages 60, 61, 85
Vivalpin: pages 74, 75

Cover layout: Jens Vogelsang

Cover photos: **XnX GmbH** and **HEAD Ski**

Barth/Brühl

Learning ... Skiing

This book is written for children just beginning to ski. The little snowman and his friend, the tiger Skitty, offer comprehensible and humorous guidance for children's first attempts on skis, to successfully skiing downhill.

In addition, the children learn interesting facts about winter sports, snow, equipment, a healthy lifestyle, and safety precautions.

136 pages, full-color print
37 photos, 240 illustrations
Paperback, 5 $^3/4$" x 8 $^1/4$"
ISBN 1-84126-154-8
£ 9.95 UK/$ 14.95 US
$ 20.95 CDN/€ 14.95

MEYER & MEYER Sport | sales@m-m-sports.com | www.m-m-sports.com

Barth/Brühl
Training ... Skiing

"Training Skiing" focuses on children and adolescents who want to train for alpine skiing. The question "Training correctly – but how?" is answered in an age-appropriate manner.

The young athletes find out how to learn the right techniques step by step, how to recognize mistakes and how to correct them. The "little Snowman" and his friend, the tiger "Skitty", are amusing companions throughout the book; they offer numerous tips on training and competing, as well as exercises to do at home.

c. 136 pages, full-color print
30 photos and 150 illustrations
Paperback, 5$^3/4$" x 8$^1/4$"
ISBN 1-84126-174-2
c. £ 9.95 UK/$ 14.95 US
$ 20.95 CDN/€ 14.90

MEYER & MEYER Sport | sales@m-m-sports.com | www.m-m-sports.com

MEYER
& MEYER
SPORT

Johannes Roschinsky

Carving
Fascination on Skis

This book describes the basics of carving
– ranging from the first steps on the flat
up to parallel skiing and on to the
special techniques for racing, having fun
and carving in deep powder snow.

It offers tips for buying the carving ski and
necessary equipment, as well as giving
tips for preparing oneself physically, and
how to avoid danger.

136 pages
Full-color print, 36 photos
16 illustrations, 18 tables
Paperback, $5^{3}/4$" x $8^{1}/4$"
ISBN 1-84126-127-0
£ 12.95 UK/$ 17.95 US
$ 25.95 CDN/€ 14.90

MEYER & MEYER Sport | sales@m-m-sports.com | www.m-m-sports.com